# Summer

by Tanya Thayer

first step nonfiction

It is summer.

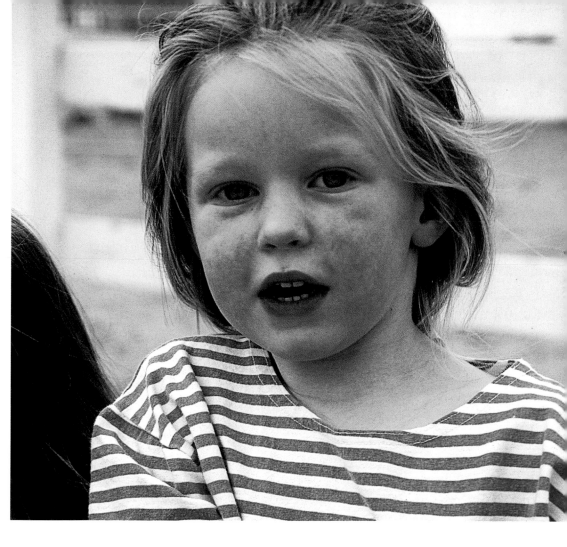

It is hot.

The days are long.

**School** is out.

Children play outside.

Families take **trips.**

Racoons learn to **hunt.**

Children learn to swim.

Goats have new **coats.**

Children wear shorts.

Dogs stay cool.

People stay cool.

Baby birds grow.

**Seeds** grow.

Children get clothes for
school.

Fall is coming.

# The Seasons

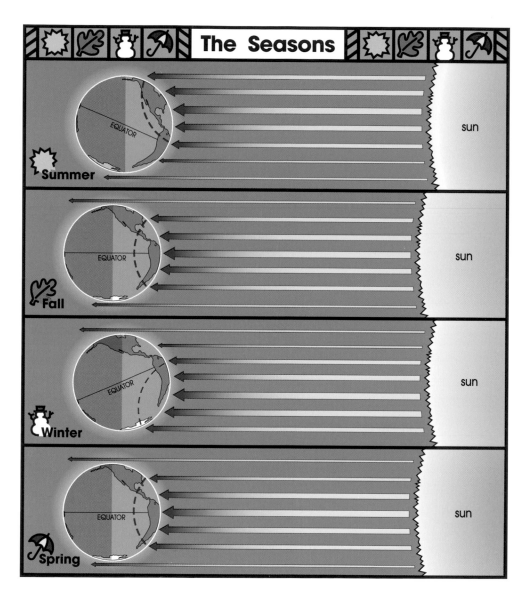

# Seasons

The earth goes around the sun.
The sun shines on the earth.
When the sun shines mostly on
the northern half of the earth, it
is summer in the United States.

There is a lot of sunlight in the
summer.  The days are longer
in the summer, too.  When
there is more sunlight in a day,
it is warmer.

# Summer Facts

In some parts of the world it feels like summer all year.

There is more daylight in the summer than there is in the spring.

Some animals lose fur in the summer. They stay cooler when they have less fur.

Sweating helps people stay cool in the summer. Panting helps some animals stay cool in the summer.

In some parts of the world it never gets dark in the summer. These places have sun even at midnight.

The bright sunlight in the summer can burn your skin. When you play outside in the summer be sure to wear a hat and sun block.

The longest day of the year is called the summer solstice. It is June 21st.

# Glossary

 **coats** – the hair covering an animal

 **hunt** – to look for food

 **seeds** – the part of a plant that can grow a new plant

 **school** – the place children go to learn

 **trips** – visits to a new place

The photographs in this book are reproduced through the courtesy of: © Stephen Graham Photography, front cover, pp. 15, 22 (middle); © Richard Cummins, p. 2; © Paulette Johnson, p. 3; © Stephen G. Donaldson, p. 4; © Jeffry W. Myers/Corbis, pp. 5, 22 (second from bottom); © Betty Crowell, p. 6; Glacial Lakes and Prairies of Northeastern South Dakota, pp. 7, 22 (bottom); © Gerald and Buff Corsi/Focus on Nature, Inc., pp. 8, 10, 22 (top and second from top); © Fukuhara, Inc. /Corbis, p 9; © Tony Arruza/Corbis, p. 11, © Norvia Behling, p. 12; © The Purcell Team/Corbis, p. 13; © Alan G. Nelson/Root Resources, p. 14; © Beth Osthoff/Independent Picture Service, p. 16; © Daniel Johnson, p. 17.

*This book is available in two editions:*
Library binding by Lerner Publications Company, a division of Lerner Publishing Group
Soft cover by First Avenue Editions, an imprint of Lerner Publishing Group
241 First Avenue North
Minneapolis, MN 55401 USA

Website address: www.lernerbooks.com


Library of Congress Cataloging-in-Publication Data

Thayer, Tanya.
    Summer / by Tanya Thayer.
        p.    cm. — (First step nonfiction)
    Includes index.
    ISBN 0-8225-1984-4 (lib. bdg. : alk. paper)
    ISBN 0-8225-1988-7 (pbk. : alk. paper)
    1. Summer—Juvenile literature. [1. Summer.] I. Title. II. Series.
QB637.6.T48 2002
508.2—dc21                                                                2001000537

Manufactured in the United States of America
  4  5  6  7  8  –  JR  –  08  07  06  05  04

# Index